Feet

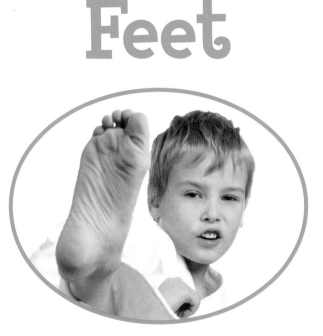

By Cynthia Klingel and Robert B. Noyed

Reading consultant: Cecilia Minden-Cupp, Ph.D.,
Adjunct Professor, College of Continuing and Professional Studies, University of Virginia

Gareth Stevens
Publishing

Please visit our Web site www.garethstevens.com. For a free color catalog of all our high-quality books, call toll free 1-800-542-2595 or fax 1-877-542-2596.

Library of Congress Cataloging-in-Publication Data

Klingel, Cynthia.
    Feet / by Cynthia Klingel and Robert B. Noyed.
      p. cm. — (Let's read about our bodies)
    Includes bibliographical references and index.
    Summary: A simple introduction to feet and their features.
    ISBN: 978-1-4339-3359-2 (lib. bdg.)
    ISBN: 978-1-4339-3360-8 (pbk.)
    ISBN: 978-1-4339-3361-5 (6-pack)
    1. Foot—Juvenile literature. [1. Foot.] I. Noyed, Robert B. II. Title.
  QM549.K54   2002
  612'.98—dc21   3564   2001054990

New edition published 2010 by
Gareth Stevens Publishing
111 East 14th Street, Suite 349
New York, NY 10003

New text and images this edition copyright © 2010 Gareth Stevens Publishing

Original edition published 2003 by Weekly Reader® Books
An imprint of Gareth Stevens Publishing
Original edition text and images copyright © 2003 Gareth Stevens Publishing

Art direction: Haley Harasymiw, Tammy Gruenewald
Page layout: Daniel Hosek, Katherine A. Goedheer
Editorial direction: Kerri O'Donnell, Diane Laska Swanke

Photo credits: Cover, pp. 9, 11 shutterstock.com; pp. 5, 7, 13, 15, 17, 19, 21 Gregg Andersen.

Printed in the United States of America

CPSIA compliance information: Batch #WW10GS: For further information contact Gareth Stevens, New York, New York at 1-800-542-2595.

Table of Contents

Boldface words appear in the glossary.

Feet Are Neat!

These are my feet!
I love my feet!

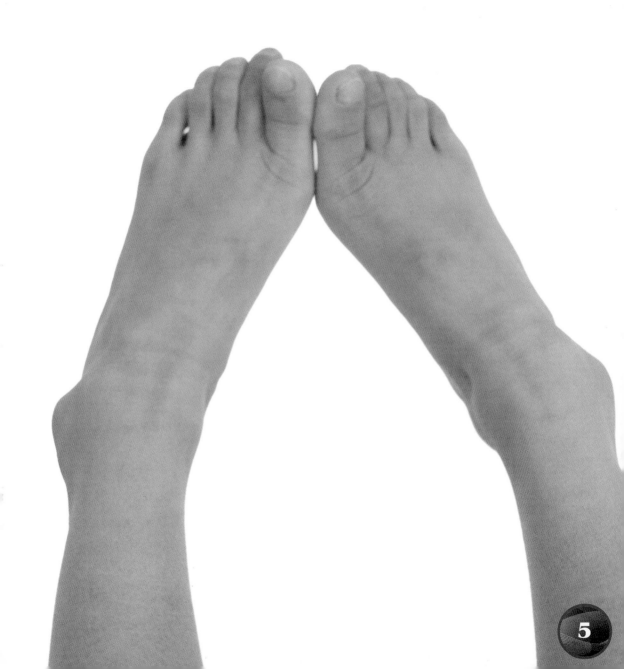

I have two feet.

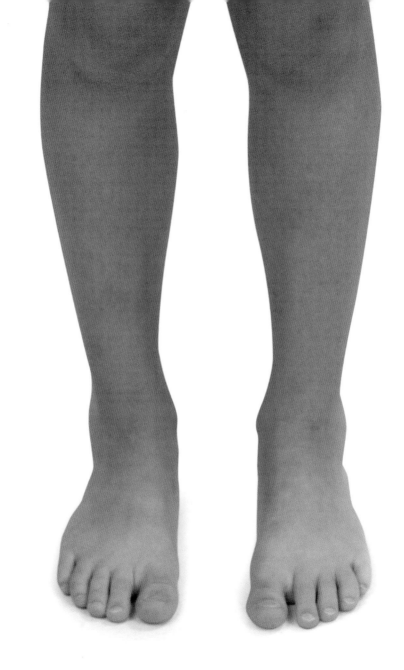

My feet are small.
Some feet are big.

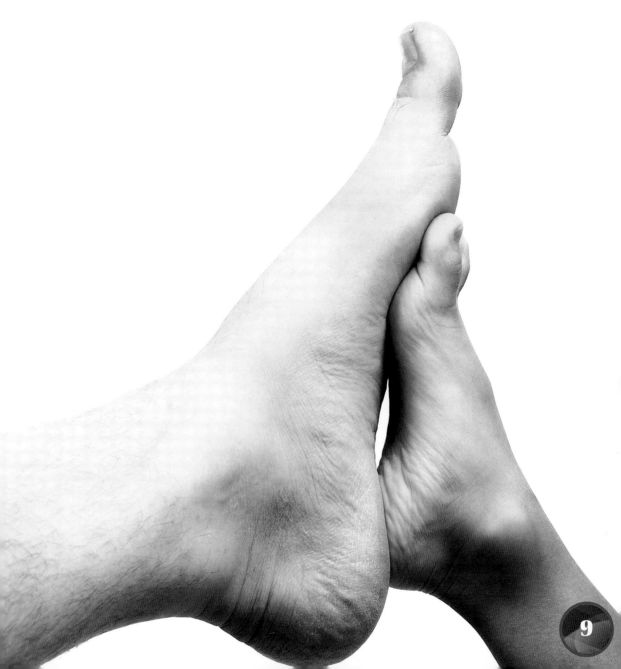

9

My feet help me walk and run. They help me jump, too!

I have ten toes.
I have five toes
on each foot.

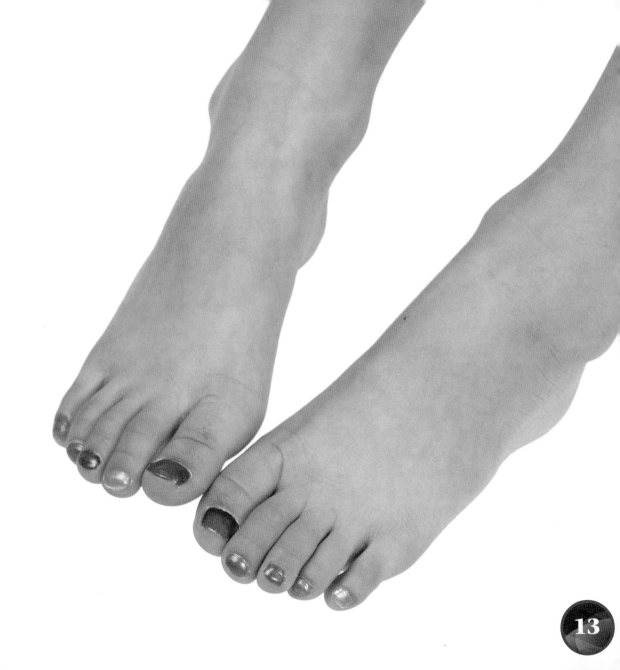

Caring for Feet

I keep my **toenails** short and **clean**.

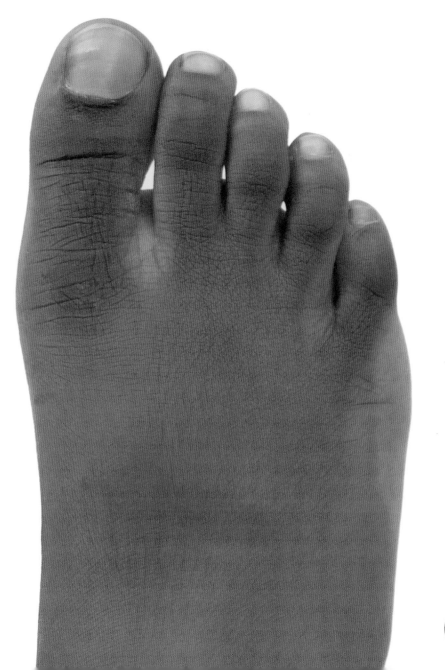

I keep my feet warm. I wear socks.

I keep my feet safe.
I wear shoes.

Feet are fun. You can **tickle** them!

Glossary

clean: to be free from dirt

tickle: to touch the body in a way that causes a tingling feeling

toenail: a thin, hard layer of material growing at the end of each toe

For More Information

Books

Douglas, Lloyd. *My Legs and Feet: My Body.* New York: Children's Press, 2004.

Hess, Nina. *Whose Feet?* New York: Random House, 2004.

Pearson, Susan. *Hooray for Feet!* Maplewood, NJ: Blue Apple Books, 2005.

Sayre, April Pulley, and Jeff Sayre. *One Is a Snail, Ten Is a Crab: A Counting by Feet Book.* Somerville, MA: Candlewick, 2006.

Sideri, Simona. *Let's Look at Feet.* Mankato, MN: Black Rabbit Books, 2004.

Web Sites

Why Does My Foot Fall Asleep?
kidshealth.org/kid/talk/qa/foot_asleep.html
For information about sleepy feet

Publisher's note to educators and parents: Our editors have carefully reviewed these Web sites to ensure that they are suitable for students. Many Web sites change frequently, however, and we cannot guarantee that a site's future contents will continue to meet our high standards of quality and educational value. Be advised that students should be closely supervised whenever they access the Internet.

Index

About the Authors

Cynthia Klingel has worked as a high school English teacher and an elementary school teacher. She is currently the curriculum director for a Minnesota school district. Cynthia Klingel lives with her family in Mankato, Minnesota.

Robert B. Noyed started his career as a newspaper reporter. Since then, he has worked in school communications and public relations at the state and national level. Robert B. Noyed lives with his family in Brooklyn Center, Minnesota.